FIREFIGHTERS

by
Jim Ollhoff

VISIT US AT:
WWW.ABDOPUBLISHING.COM

Editor: John Hamilton
Graphic Design: Sue Hamilton
Cover Design: Neil Klinepier
Cover Photo: iStockphoto
Interior Photos and Illustrations: Alamy-pg 25; AP-pgs 20 (inset top), 22, 24 & 28;
Corbis-pgs 16, 18, 19, 21 & 29; Glow Images-pgs 13 & 17; Granger Collection-pg 7;
iStockphoto-pgs 9, 15, 26 & 27; John Hamilton-pgs 4 & 32; Thinkstock-pgs 1, 3, 5, 6 &
11; Photo Researchers-pg 20 (bottom); US Forest Service/California Smokejumpers-pg 23.

ABDO Booklinks
To learn more about Emergency Workers, visit ABDO Publishing Company online.
Web sites about Emergency Workers are featured on our Book Links pages. These links
are routinely monitored and updated to provide the most current information available.
Web site: www.abdopublishing.com

Library of Congress Cataloging-in-Publication Data

Ollhoff, Jim, 1959-
  Firefighter / Jim Ollhoff.
     p. cm. -- (Emergency workers)
  Audience: 10-14
  Includes index.
  ISBN 978-1-61783-513-1
  1. Fire fighters--Juvenile literature. I. Title.
  TH9148.O45 2013
  363.37--dc23
                        2012005328

TABLE OF CONTENTS

FIREFIGHTERS

The job of a firefighter can be both exciting and dangerous. Fire is unpredictable. Winds sometimes cause flames to spread to neighboring buildings. Flammable materials can explode, causing serious damage or injury. Firefighters must always be on guard.

Despite the danger, firefighters have a very rewarding career. They work to help people, whether they are putting out house fires or rescuing someone from

Firefighters cut holes in the roof of a home to control a house fire.

a burning building. They might give first aid to fire victims, or cut away twisted metal at a car accident to free trapped passengers. Firefighters are in the business of helping people and saving lives.

On any day, firefighters may have to risk their lives to save others. This career requires a lot of courage and dedication.

FIREFIGHTING HISTORY

Community firefighting dates back to the Roman Empire, and possibly even to ancient Egypt. In ancient Rome, hundreds of people called "watchmen" patrolled the streets of the city. If they found an out-of-control fire, they lined up and passed buckets of water, hand-to-hand, to try to extinguish the blaze.

In the Middle Ages in Europe, fire was a constant danger. Most houses were made of wood. They often had roofs made of dry vegetation like reeds or straw. Most people needed a fire pit in their home for cooking and warmth, but it could quickly turn dangerous. Most villages couldn't afford full-time firefighters, but the citizens made emergency plans. For example, the village butcher might be responsible for bringing a useful ax to a house fire, while the carpenter brought a ladder, and the barrel-maker brought buckets.

Firefighters in London in the 1800s.

In North America, fire wardens first appeared in the early 1600s. In 1736, Benjamin Franklin organized a volunteer fire service in Philadelphia, Pennsylvania. Firefighters and their equipment continued to improve over the next few hundred years. Unfortunately, it sometimes took a catastrophic fire before communities took steps to organize their firefighters and buy proper equipment.

Benjamin Franklin organized and became chief of the Union Fire Company, a volunteer fire service in Philadelphia, Pennsylvania.

KINDS OF FIRES

A few hundred years ago, water was the only thing firefighters needed to douse a blaze. Today, there are so many different kinds of materials that burn, and so many different kinds of fires, that it takes much more knowledge and skill to be a firefighter.

Firefighters today must deal with several "classes," or types, of fire. A fire's class depends on what kind of material is burning.

CLASS A

Class A fires are fueled by paper, cloth, and wood. This includes most house fires. They are usually put out with water.

CLASS B

Class B fires are fueled by flammable liquids, such as gasoline or paint. These fires are often put out with carbon dioxide, which robs the fire of the oxygen it needs to burn. If someone tried to put out a Class B fire with water, it could make the fire worse.

CLASS C

Class C fires start because of an electrical problem. Electrical fires are usually put out with carbon dioxide or a dry chemical.

CLASS D

Class D fires start with fuel from unusual metals, such as magnesium or titanium. They need to be extinguished with special chemicals that smother the flames. Water on a Class D fire can make the fire worse.

CLASS K

Class K fires involve cooking oils, grease, or other fats. These fires are usually extinguished with special chemicals.

CLASSES OF FIRES	TYPES OF FIRES	PICTURE SYMBOL
A	Wood, paper, cloth, and other ordinary materials.	
B	Gasoline, oil, paint, and other flammable liquids.	
C	Fires involving live electrical equipment.	
D	Flammable metals and metal alloys, such as magnesium and titanium.	
K	Cooking media such as vegetable or animal oils and fats.	

WHAT DOES A FIREFIGHTER DO?

When firefighters are on their way to a fire, they never know exactly what they'll have to do once they arrive. They might have to give emergency medical aid to someone who is injured. They might have to rescue victims from a burning building. They might have to search for people who are missing.

Firefighters are often the first to arrive on a scene that may involve hazardous materials, such as poisons spewing into the air. Firefighters need to know how to respond.

Firefighters might have to cut holes in the roof of a house fire to let out heat or smoke. They might have to carry heavy fire hoses up long flights of stairs to extinguish a blaze.

When firefighters are not fighting fires, they need to prepare to fight the next one. They need to stay physically fit. They need to stay educated about fire suppression and safety. They have to check their equipment, and get it ready for the next alarm. They must be ready on a moment's notice. When it comes to fighting fires, every second counts.

Firefighters never know what they might have to do when they respond to a call.

FIREFIGHTER TRAINING

People who want to be firefighters need to graduate from high school. They go through a background check, and have to pass a physical test to make sure they can endure the rigors of firefighting. They apply to become a firefighter at a local fire department, usually by filling out an application and taking a test. If accepted, they go through the fire department academy, which includes two to four months of full-time classes and training.

During training, they learn all the parts of being a good firefighter. They learn fire science, and how to extinguish different kinds of fires. They learn how to drive and operate fire trucks. They learn basic medical information and rescue techniques.

Firefighters-in-training go through live fire exercises. Fire departments sometimes have buildings that they can burn, or they find buildings that are going to be destroyed anyway. The building is set on fire, and the student firefighters, under direction from an instructor, have to put it out.

Firefighters train at a live-fire exercise. They must be very physically fit to be able to lift heavy hoses, or rescue people who have been overcome by smoke.

Good health and physical fitness are very important to firefighters. They need to lift heavy hoses, and may need to carry injured people. They have to crawl through tight spaces and move quickly, all while wearing heavy equipment and protective clothing. Firefighters need to always be physically fit, so they are ready to exert themselves when needed.

One of the most important parts of firefighting is something that can't always be taught. Firefighters need to be calm and cool under pressure. They need the courage to risk their own lives to save others. They need to calmly listen to directions and take orders when fire is raging all around them. They need to be able to solve unusual problems quickly as they figure out how to save lives and property. Firefighters who panic or get too nervous might easily injure themselves or others.

5

FIREFIGHTING EQUIPMENT

Firefighters wear protective equipment that sometimes weighs up to 50 pounds (23 kg). The equipment includes safety boots, pants, jacket, helmet, and gloves. These items protect the firefighter from a fire's intense heat. Firefighters wear a breathing tank called a SCBA (self-contained breathing apparatus) so they can breathe clean air instead of the toxic smoke that results from fires. Firefighters also carry two-way radios to communicate with each other.

There are many tools stored in fire trucks. An ax may be used to break through doors and walls. A halligan bar has a pick and a wedge on the end. It is useful for breaking into places or pulling or striking things.

A firefighter holds an ax, with a halligan bar next to him.

Firefighters have their gear ready to go.

FORD N GIORDANO S KLINE B

Fire trucks carry hydraulic rescue tools, sometimes called the "jaws of life." These are often used after automobile accidents, when twisted metal prevents car doors from opening. The jaws of life cut through the twisted metal so that victims can be rescued and get medical attention.

Firefighters are usually first on the scene of hazardous material incidents. They might face poisonous chemical spills, or tanker truck crashes involving toxic substances. Firefighters carry specialized equipment to deal with the hazardous material.

Firefighters might also carry a thermal imaging camera. It is a device that detects heat. In a burning building, thick smoke often makes it impossible to see. The thermal imaging camera can help a firefighter find the heat of an unconscious victim, or see the main source of a fire. It can also be used to find smoldering ashes, so firefighters could extinguish a fire before it gets out of control.

A thermal imaging camera shows a person enveloped in heavy smoke.

A firefighter uses the "jaws of life" to open a jammed car door.

FIRE ENGINES

A fire engine does a lot more than just transport firefighters to a fire. It's an important tool

A brush truck allows firefighters to travel through rough terrain.

for fighting fires. There are many different kinds of fire trucks. Depending on the community, fire stations might have fireboats or fire airplanes, too. If a community is surrounded by a lot of wilderness or forests, they might have a brush truck, which allows for off-road travel.

Some fire trucks include an onboard water tank so firefighters can spray water immediately. Usually, firefighters have to hook hoses from a fire hydrant to the truck. The water then flows from the truck to another hose. Running water through the truck allows firefighters to manage water pressure. Some fire trucks inject foam into the water, which makes it more effective in extinguishing certain kinds of fires.

A fireboat puts out a fire on a dock.

One of the most recognizable
fire engines includes a giant ladder
that can extend very high. This is called a
turntable ladder. It can be used for rescuing
people in high buildings, or lifting a firefighter
high enough to spray water from on top of a blaze.

DIFFERENT KINDS OF FIREFIGHTERS

Many different kinds of people are firefighters, and firefighters have many different kinds of jobs. Some firefighters are volunteers. That means they don't get paid for their firefighting work. They have regular jobs, just like everyone else. But when their phone or beeper goes off, they have to drop everything and rush to the firehouse to get their equipment and run off to the fire.

Other firefighters are paid to stay at the firehouse. They are always on-call, waiting for a fire. They eat and sleep at the firehouse, knowing that at any minute a call could come through to go to a fire. Sometimes they work for 24 hours in a single shift.

Some firefighters work at airports. Others work in factories. Some are stationed in forests, watching for forest fires.

Firefighters put out a fire in a cargo plane.

When there is a forest fire, or a fire in a remote wilderness area, special firefighters called smoke jumpers are called in. They are flown or driven into the fire area. They sometimes chop down trees to try to take away a fire's fuel.

Above: A smoke jumper parachutes into a remote area where a fire has broken out.
Below: A smoke jumper digs away the underbrush, robbing the fire of fuel.

A fire investigator looks for the cause of a building fire.

Sometimes, a fire has a suspicious origin. People wonder how it started. Was it by accident? Did someone fall asleep and leave a candle burning? Did someone commit arson, which means they started a fire on purpose? Answering these questions is a job for the fire investigator. The fire investigator is like a detective who looks through the ruins of a building and figures out how a fire started.

A California fire inspector checks out a fireworks booth for safety before it opens to the public.

Fire marshals and fire inspectors work to prevent fires. They inspect buildings to make sure all rooms have at least two ways out. They warn building owners about unsafe practices, like piling boxes in front of exit doors. They work with city planners and builders to make sure that buildings are safe from fire. Fire marshals may also be government officials or law enforcement officers. Without fire marshals and inspectors, more people would be injured, or killed, from many more fires.

INTERVIEW WITH A FIREFIGHTER

Tina is a firefighter and 911 dispatcher from southern Minnesota. She is also trained as an Emergency Medical Technician and a Hazardous Materials Technician. Her father was a firefighter, so she spent lots of time at the fire hall growing up. She is the mother of two boys, and her husband is also a firefighter and an EMT.

Q: How did you get interested in firefighting?

Tina: My father and uncle have been involved in firefighting since I was little, so I have been around firefighters for a long time. I spent a lot of time at the fire hall as a child. I dated a firefighter and one of our mutual friends suggested that I join, so I did and loved it.

A young girl visits a fire station and tries on firefighting equipment.

Q: What's an average day like as a firefighter?

Tina: Since I'm a volunteer, my day begins like many other people's days. Volunteers get up in the morning, drink coffee, get ready for work, and spend time with our families. But at any time we can be called to action, regardless of what we are currently doing. We could be sleeping, eating dinner, or taking a shower. Many times a home-cooked meal or family celebration has been interrupted by my pager going off.

Volunteer firefighters must be ready to go to work at any time of the day or night.

27

Q: What's your most memorable experience as a firefighter?

Tina: I have many good memories of being a firefighter, most of all the gratefulness of the people you help. Even when people go through traumatic events, such as a house fire, they are always thankful we were there to help them. I think many people become firefighters because they care about others and want to help their community.

Q: What's the best part about being a firefighter?

Tina: The best part of being a firefighter is the bond you develop with your colleagues. They become like your brothers and sisters and you care about them as you would your own family. You rely on these people to watch out for you when you are on calls with them and you in turn watch over them.

Q: What advice would you have for someone who wants to be a firefighter when they grow up?

Tina: Work hard on your education. Get good grades and maintain physical fitness. Visit the local fire station when they have open houses or other community events. Join a local firefighter explorer program if available. Always practice fire safety!

On and off duty, firefighters depend on and take care of each other.

29

GLOSSARY

ARSON

The illegal act of intentionally starting a fire to destroy a building.

CATASTROPHIC

Terrible danger that is often sudden or unexpected, which typically leads to great losses of life and property.

EMERGENCY MEDICAL TECHNICIAN (EMT)

A person trained to provide emergency first aid to victims before and while being taken to a hospital.

FIRE INSPECTOR

A firefighter who works to prevent fires by inspecting the safety of buildings and approving the fire safety plans of newly constructed buildings. May also be called a fire marshal.

FIRE INVESTIGATOR

A firefighter who looks through the ruins of a burned building to figure out how a fire started.

FLAMMABLE

Something that is easily set on fire, such as gasoline or paint.

Hugh Halligan holds his invention, the halligan bar.

Halligan instructs firefighters on how to use the halligan bar to pry open a door.

HALLIGAN BAR

A tool used by fire and rescue personnel with a fork on one end, and a blade and a pick on the other. The bar was designed in 1948 by Hugh Halligan of the New York Fire Department. The halligan bar is used for prying open building and vehicle doors, breaking out walls and windows, and many other purposes.

HAZARDOUS MATERIALS TECHNICIAN

A person trained to clean up hazardous waste accidents and spills, such as chemical or nuclear waste.

HYDRAULIC RESCUE TOOL

A pneumatic tool (operated by pressurized gas or air) used by firefighters and other rescue personnel to cut away metal, such as a car door, to free a trapped victim. Also known as the "jaws of life."

SELF-CONTAINED BREATHING APPARTUS (SCBA)

An air tank and breathing mask that is worn by firefighters. The SCBA allows them to breathe their own clean air supply while moving through smoke- and gas-filled buildings.

INDEX